There is No THEM

Praise for There is No THEM

"Open your heart and soul by devouring this cherishable book."

— Mark Victor Hansen, co-creator of the #1 New York
Times best-selling series, *Chicken Soup for the Soul*

"Every once in a while, a story can change the lives of millions.
Profound and brilliantly crafted, the insights in this book are
both spiritual and practical. I urge every parent and teen to read
this book together to help cement a bond that will never die. A
timeless classic for the struggle we face collectively, and will face
again alone."

— Robert G. Allen, author of the New York Times best
sellers *No Money Down, Creating Wealth, Multiple Streams
of Income* and the forthcoming *One Minute Millionaire*

"Dawn Holman's *There is No THEM* is a powerfully compelling
story of compassion and the search for life's deeper meanings."

— Patricia Morgan, author of *Love Her As She Is*

"Dawn Holman has written this great book for all of us, and
especially for those who work with and love young people. My
suggestion is to buy at least 12 copies. *There is No THEM* is the
perfect gift for those who are distraught or downhearted and
need inspiring, enriching yet practical ideas to hang onto and use.
It is a recipe, a road map, and most of all, a friend."

— Dottie Walters, author of *Speak & Grow Rich*
President, Walters International Speakers Bureau
Publisher/Editor, *Sharing IDEAS* Speakers Magazine

There is No THEM

a boy, a stranger and life's greatest lesson

Dawn M. Holman

UNCAGED
PRODUCTIONS

There is No THEM

published by UNCAGED PRODUCTIONS
1 (866) 862-2438

Copyright © 2001 by Dawn M. Holman
International Standard Book Number:
0-9730588-0-3

Cover Design by Kevin Franco
Illustrations and Logo by Alexandra Morris, age 17
www.cheezrulez.com

ATTENTION
Organizations, Schools and Corporate "Champions"

This book was created to be a fundraiser or distributed as
a client and/or community service. It is available at
substantial quantity discounts for community and
educational initiatives, or business sales/promotional use.

For immediate processing of individual orders,
anytime 7 days a week call: 1 (800) 431-1579

Printed and bound in Canada   First Edition

Acknowledgements

There is No THEM is dedicated to
the future adults of this world and
to all who love them.

Special Thanks

A special acknowledgement to Alexandra Morris for
her artistic interpretation at every turn of the page.
Her poignant symbolism sheds light on the silent
story within, in a way that only the heart of a
17-year-old could see. What a bright delight you are!
My deep appreciation to Kevin Lanuke for his
enthusiastic support of publishing to raise monies
for community and educational causes.
To Lyle Manery for his direction in securing
corporate "champions" to further support the
end beneficiaries of this book. To my family and
friends for your patience and support as the
message and its mission evolved. And to all
the readers and listeners of my previous works
and programs who took the time to write and call,
and planted the seeds for greater things to come.

Preface

In times of uncertainty, reassurance can
come in unexpected ways.

This story is inspired by a chance encounter with
a young man and his all too soon experience
with the reminders of life's fragility.

Like a hot flame licking the palm of my hand,
his questions tortured me until I opened the door to
There is No THEM. His face haunted my soul as if
to say: "What if our time together could help others
who need to hear a story about the power of the
unsinkable soul that is ours to claim in this lifetime?"

Who am I to deny expression of his challenge and
gift to me? Who are any of us to deny
our individual contributions to the world?

That's why I deeply believe we did not meet
by chance, as with so many things along the way
that alter our lives forever. Perhaps it is no
coincidence either that you are holding this book
in your hands. Maybe it is to serve as a nudge
for you to practice what you already know,
or maybe it's time for you to show
the world your gift, too.

For whatever reason you have picked up
this little book, it is my heartfelt hope that
it unleashes in you the power of your greatness.

"The tragedy of life is not death,
but what we let die inside of us
while we live."

— *Norman Cousins*

"To be what we are,
and to become what we are
capable of becoming,
is the only end to life."

— *Robert Louis Stevenson*

"We must be the change
we want to see in the world."

— *Gandi*

*I*t was early Monday morning toward the middle of September. Brent lay sleeping unaware of his mother's departure. It had been her habit these past nine months to tuck a special card under his pillow, before she left for work on Monday mornings.

*A*s a corporate trainer, she helped executives organize their time to be more productive and often flew from city to city. Yet hidden beneath her seminar message, there was an underlying belief she secretly held about time.

She often mused that humans were stressed because they are the only creatures who wear watches. Ask any cat or dog. They just know when their human is coming home. No need for such devices to record time. And always happy to see us because somehow they took to heart that familiar greeting, "Have a nice day." Maybe that's why each time she boarded a flight home, she took off her watch and then broke out in a defiant little grin.

*O*n this particular morning, Brent looked more angelic than his usual 17-year-old self. His flaxen curls offset by a dark blue pillow, like a field of sunlit straw lapping at the ocean. The rest of his body, however, was a different matter. Legs sprawled across the bed, pointing both east and west like a confused weathervane. The energy of youth going in all directions at once.

And so it was, like any other Monday morning, that his mother bent over to kiss his sleeping forehead and locked the door behind her.

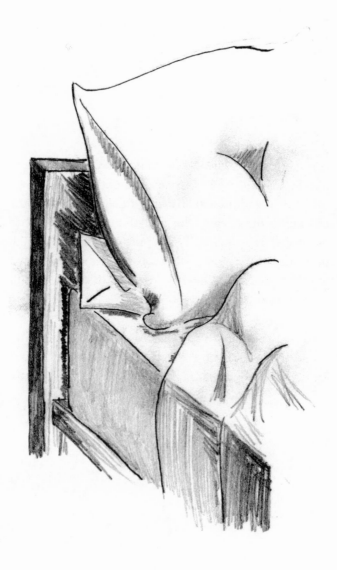

*B*y the time Brent woke at 7:45, she was already in the air. He enjoyed a free and easy relationship with his mom, but at times it did get lonely. Even though the agreed routine was that she organize her workshops so that she was out of town only every second week. But then, there were always the cards. So he lifted the pillow for a peek in lieu of a "good morning" hug.

*W*ith a smile he leapt into the warmth of the shower. As his eyes adjusted to the brightness of the bathroom lighting, his hunger woke up too. He bolted to the kitchen for his usual morning concoction — chocolate-flavored protein power, frozen strawberries, banana and whatever else happened to catch his eye fit for the brew.

A few minutes later, the buzz of the dryer. Clean clothes for the week. As a young child, Brent had always liked the warmth of just dried clothes. He grabbed his laundry, crumpled it into a ball against his bare chest and flew up the stairs... then tucked in his still warm shirt and stuffed his mother's card into one of his schoolbooks.

*A*n hour later he looked as if he'd fallen back to sleep. Slouched in his seat during a history class, he glanced to make sure that no one was watching and pulled out the card.

Sneaking a peek became a private little game of his and on more than one occasion he disrupted the class by snickering out loud before he could catch his reaction. His mother had an eye for spotting zany cards that made him laugh, often at the very things that were bugging him. Brent saved his favorite ones.

On this particular day, the teacher was already on to him and glancing in his direction. So it was much too obvious to pull the card out its envelope. But his mother, as if she somehow knew he would be foiled this time, had also enclosed a cartoon clipping that peeked out just over the edge. Brent deftly slipped it into his palm and stole a look. He looked out the window and grinned undefeated.

_B_rent's mom always called on Monday evenings when she was out of town. She loved to tease him into a bout of friendly banter. She called that evening too, but he stayed late at the library to finish a school project and then went to the gym. By the time Brent got home all he could do was crash into bed. The clean clothes that started the day lay crumpled on the floor below.

Meanwhile, his mom had left a message: "Just checking in between meetings. If it's not too late when I get back to the hotel, I'll try again. Otherwise, I'll call tomorrow. Oh, and did the towel tyrant like his card and cartoon? Catch you later sport. Love ya."

*T*wo weeks later, Brent was the one boarding a plane on a Monday morning. That's when I met him.

As I spotted my seat, I had half a minute to observe my companion for this flight. Although there seemed a bit of mystery to him, I liked him without really knowing why and so I smiled.

I moved down the aisle toward him. The plane began to feel tomb-like. It was almost two-thirds empty. And although I would have loved the unexpected opportunity to stretch out across the seats, I felt a strange comfort in the fact that passengers were paired in rows, two-by-two, like Noah's ark.

*B*rent sat by the window. I was in the aisle. The seat in the middle was empty. He looked lonely, yet fearful of bridging the distance between us despite his muscular appearance. He had a torturous mix of anger on his face and sadness in his eyes. Yet I sensed he wanted to talk, so I waited for just the right moment — when he pushed away his tray of airline food, untouched.

"You might get hungry by the end of the trip. How about a protein bar? It's one of the better tasting ones."

He carefully read the ingredients. To my delight, 32 grams of protein in a special blend of linoleic acid, dietary fiber and complex carbohydrates seemed to suit his taste.

"Thanks," he said quietly.

After he swallowed his first mouthful, he recognized that it might be polite to start up a bit of conversation. So with half a smile he said, "You're not a body builder, are you?"

"No, I just eat like one," I quipped.

*A*nd with that reply whatever need he had to talk was satisfied. There was no introduction, not another exchange. So I decided to give it one more shot and asked, "What else interests you besides protein bars?"

"Not much. Don't feel much like talking either." He paused and then said, "Sorry."

"That's okay. I have days like that too. There's nothing worse than being trapped beside someone who wants to talk your ear off when you're not up to it. But if you want some more of these, I have a few extra bars stashed away. And by the way, my name is Dawn."

"Mine's Brent," he said with his arms still frozen in a quasi hug over his torso. He turned his head and looked out the window.

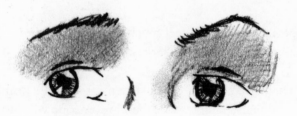

The sunlight filtered through the edges of his blonde hair, creating a sharp contrast with the black sports sweater he was wearing. His eyes were a brew of gold and brown, like a fine blend of sun-kissed coffee beans. The kind of eyes I would have liked a child of mine to have. Yet the angry set of his jaw would have made me uncomfortable, had it been someone else.

I resumed reading my book, an inspirational fiction. Eleven pages later, I felt Brent's eyes peering at the cover. My silent agreement to respect his wish of non-conversation must have earned his trust, given him a sense of permission to "just be." And for whatever reason, that silence broke a barrier. That's when his pain erupted out loud.

"Just tell me one thing! Why, why do people, innocent people, have to die like that?"

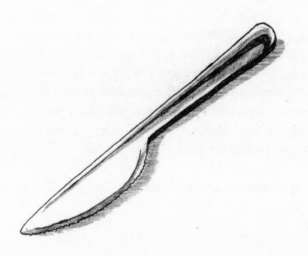

ou could have heard a plastic knife drop. He quickly buried his face to hide from the deafening silence that suddenly fell throughout the plane.

In an instinctive attempt to protect him I quietly said, "I don't really know exactly. But if you'd like to talk a bit, maybe we can make some sense of it."

*A*ll of a sudden his manly chest seemed out of place with the child-like expression in his eyes. "Well my mom, my mom was about your age. She um…What do you do?"

"I've had quite a diverse career, yet all the pieces have come together quite miraculously into one key focus. I help people get unstuck so they can move forward to live more powerful lives. And what about you? What do you enjoy doing?"

"Not much lately. But I used to go to the gym a lot. And I'm on my high school debating team."

"I admire teens with the courage to stand up and be counted for who they are. Especially when they haven't let their lens on the world get distorted by adult views on life. So, how are you going to apply that brilliant mind of yours?"

He sighed.

"I'm 18 next summer. In my last year of high school now. I was planning to go into business like my, my mom. She was one of the best in her field, you know. She had scholarships all the way through university, worked real hard too. She didn't come from a very wealthy family, but she sure made up for it later on… And then, what did she get for it!"

Brent's shoulders started to shake. He swallowed deep to stop the tears.

"They tell you to study hard, get a good education so you can earn lots of money to have what you want in life, and then you die before you have a chance to enjoy it. What's the use if you're going to get snuffed out like that? Tell me! What's the use?

"For all I know, that could be me some day. Just going about my business and then, BOOM, it's all over. Just like that."

Brent snapped his fingers.

"My mother didn't deserve that. She was just visiting the World Trade Center. Just visiting!"

*A*ll heads turned in our direction. All eyes fell on me wondering what I was going to say to this angry young man who was hurting so badly on the inside there was no place left for him to hide. I reached deeper than deep, to my very core, in search of an answer. Now, it was my turn to swallow hard.

"Brent, no one deserves to die a horrible death. And you don't deserve to have your mother taken away from you like that, to be left with all this pain. And I'm not saying that just because I'm an adult, I could handle it any better than you.

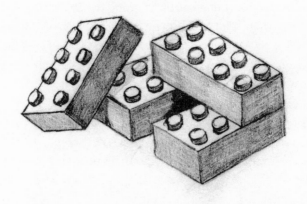

"But giving up is not the answer. You can quit whatever you want in life. No one can get inside your head and order your thoughts around. You're the only one who really has a vote. You can even give up on your dreams and sleep walk through life, if you like. But ask yourself whether it makes any sense to cause your own pain, by tearing yourself apart rather than building yourself back up? Life is like a continuous construction project, one day's work at a time.

"I realize it's very difficult to step back from everything that's happened right now. But I think we can find another way to look at things, maybe even make some sense of what seems senseless, if we quiet our minds and take ourselves to another time and place. Would you allow me to guide your thoughts for a few minutes?"

"Okay."

"Close your eyes and imagine the one place that always makes you feel very safe and calm. That special place that feels like no other place on earth. See it. Feel it. Hear it. Smell it. I'm not asking you to share it with me. Just nod when you get there."

His shoulders relaxed a bit and his breathing slowed. Then he nodded.

"You said your mother was the best in her field. I think she was a leader of something much greater than that. This may be more spiritual than you're ready to hear right now. But on some level, she chose to be part of that collective group of men and women who gave up their lives that day. Men and women of extraordinary strength and courage."

"That's okay, I leafed through a few of those kinds of books when mom used to leave them lying around the house," he said with a slight smile that lasted a nanosecond before the next cloud passed by.

I leaned closer to escape the blinding reflection as the wing began to catch the midday sun. Suddenly a halo of light seemed to appear around his head.

"*B*rent, what I'm trying to say is that I don't think your mother would think of herself as a victim. I see her as a leader. There was purpose and meaning to her death. Most of us go through life looking to other people for leadership — to those we think are in power. But your mother, and others with her that day, recognized that there was no 'them'. So they claimed their own power and became 'them'. They took responsibility for an entire nation that fell asleep.

The rest of us were spared to continue the course correction they started. We can't go back to the way we were after this. When all is said and done, you and your children will have a better world to live in because of it."

"Mankind must put an end to war.... ..Or war will put an end to Mankind"

– John F. Kennedy

*B*rent's eyes widened. "Is that why all the talk shows are going on about waking up to what really matters?"

"Yes. Not since the assassination of John F. Kennedy have we all simultaneously gasped, 'Oh My God!' We froze in disbelief, as if we were watching a movie. Only this time our mortality was stamped collectively on our foreheads, as plain as the expiry date on a carton of milk. People have been hit with the realization that their lives could be taken away in an instant. That there are no guarantees, even though there never were any. September 11th turned the volume up on the message. Shattered our illusion of control so we had to stop and listen.

"The fact is sometimes it's easy to lose sight of the things that really matter and we take for granted the preciousness of our seemingly imperfect lives. Some of us even forgot to take time to participate in it, living by a schedule as if it were divine law.

"*I*t's kind of like being asked to clean up your room. You keep letting things pile up and pile up, until one day it all comes crashing down on you. Life can be like that too, if you don't pay attention.

"It also woke up our compassion for the suffering around us. We used to look at the turmoil in other parts of the world and wonder what it had to do with our life. We've never really experienced such devastation on our own soil before. Now we see. We've made the connection. And the lesson will be wasted, unless we hold onto that connection.

"As a result the whole emotional landscape of North America, and perhaps the world, has changed. Ultimately, I think what happened will contribute to world peace. And your mother is part of all that."

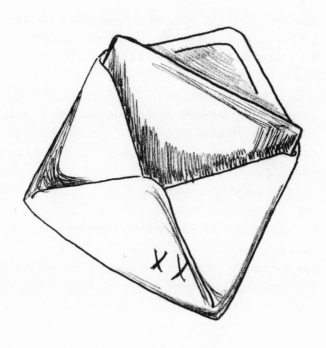

*F*or the first time Brent managed half a smile. Then I said, "I sense that you and your mom had a good relationship."

"Yeah", he said softly. His body drew inward making him look like a little boy again. I thought he was about to crawl under his seat and then I realized he was just reaching down to grab his knapsack. He pulled out a bright blue envelope.

"My mom always left me Monday cards, ever since her best friend died of cancer a year ago. But since this happened I haven't been able to read her last card to me. Would you, um?"

Tears began streaming down his face.

Good Morning Brent!

I wish I were there to see your face with this one. Between the picture on the card and the cartoon, it kind of says it all!

I bet that's the last time you'll leave your towels soaking wet on the bathroom floor! But then having a perfect son would be rather boring, don't ya think? So I guess it's best to love you just the way you are.

Besides, if you grow up too fast, you'll only have more time to miss being a teenager. And speaking of that, thanks for letting me in on your party this weekend. Most sons would have interpreted my unexpected return as "Mom crashing the party." But not you sport. You know how to roll with the punches.

Well, got to toss your grungy socks into the laundry. But just in case you're too partied out and sleep through your alarm, I left one pair on your night table to bring you around... Whew! Didn't think I was going to let you off scot-free for the mess in the bathroom, now did you?

You know I don't like leaving you on my "fly weeks" but I love it when I find something to kick off your Mondays. Hugs till I return. I'll call tonight.

Lots of Love,
Mom

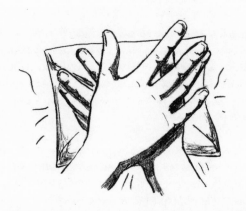

*T*his was one of the most difficult things I've ever had to do. The anxiety of not knowing what might be a mother's last words to her son. Thank God for both of us they were in character, through and through, with how she lived and the relationship they had.

Brent made no motion to read the card himself. So I carefully tucked it away inside its bright blue envelope that read, "Gotcha This Time, Sport!" I placed it on his lap. He reached with his hand and slid the envelope up toward his chest, pressing it tightly as if to never let it go.

I felt his emptiness in the pit of my stomach.

*A*fter what seemed an eternity he became unexpectedly calm and looked at me, really looked at me, for the first time. "I guess there are some things we'll never know in life?"

At that moment I saw a glimpse of the man he would be. "That's true. And there are some things you'll want to forget in life and not know, too."

"Tell me some of the things you still don't know," he said.

"That will take longer than this flight, but I can tell you some of the biggest questions I still have about life. In the work I used to do, I sat at the bedside of many people who died with regrets. Often because they gave up their lives trying to prove themselves to the world. Constantly looking for ways to make themselves look good on the outside to feel good on the inside. Never realizing that all the while they always were 'enough'. That strength grows from the inside out.

"Being a witness to this haunted me so I began asking questions such as: Why do we live as if we're never going to die and then die, afraid to let go, as if we've never had the chance to live? Why do we even need a wake-up call in the first place? What really gets in the way of being the person we want to be, or living the life we deserve? What happens to that fearless sense of adventure we have as a child to explore our world with curiosity, free from the worry of who might be watching us? Is it that a child knows no fear until we teach it fear, no limits until we teach it limits? Is that why adults get caught up in a cycle of struggle and lack?

"But Brent, I can assure you after reading your mom's letter that she didn't leave this earth with the kind of heavy regrets I've felt with others. Every day she said what was in her heart. She died as she lived. She left you with a smile and a hug, not open wounds. And a bond that will last forever."

"I guess, in a way, I'm glad my mother experienced death with her friend," said Brent. "After Sharon died of cancer, that's when mom started writing me Monday cards. To kind of start off my week on the right foot, especially the weeks she was working away from home.

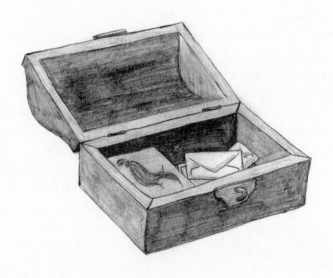

"And then last December, mom had this special wooden box made up with a fancy brass plaque that had one of her favorite sayings and my name engraved on it. She put a whole series of letters in there. Letters to open on my 21st birthday, when I graduated from university, when I got married, had my first baby. And other times like when I was thinking of making a career change or having a tough time in my marriage, even one for my 80th birthday. She also put in some of her favorite books and told me how they helped her through difficult times in her life. And some poems she wrote when she was younger. Even a lock of her hair."

"*D*id she tell you why she made up this special box for you?"

"In a way. She sat on the floor with me after I opened it. We talked for a long time. It was the first time we ever really talked about death and about the purpose and meaning of life. She told me that when she died she wanted me to go on living, to be thankful for what we shared together. And not to be sad for too long because it would be sadder if I robbed the other people in my life of what I have to offer. Because she said each day of our life was a gift not to be taken for granted.

"She also said she wanted me to do what makes me happy and to approach life like an explorer. And on days when I can't get excited about being alive, to do it for her because she will always be watching over me. Not to wish even one day of my life away because you never know when it could be your last. She said we're all just leasing time. That we only think we can own it by trying to manage it, but we can't.

"She made me promise to remember to be part of my family's day, every day, when I have kids. She said I was her biggest joy and that one day I will understand because my kids will be my biggest joy too. And that I'll also have more to give to them, if I do what I love to do rather than work at a job for the sake of money. That it's best to do something that really expresses who I am."

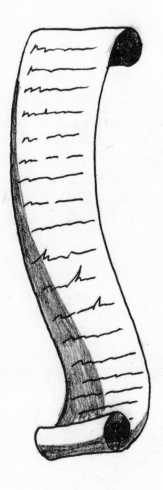

"Your mother was very wise, Brent. Most of us aren't that prepared. Some of us, like your mother's friend, have the gift of knowing that we're going to die soon so we have one last chance to pack in as much as we can and say what needs to be said before we check out. But too many of us forget what really matters, until it's too late. Usually it's not intentional. It's by default.

"The toughest part for you is making the transition from a physical to a spiritual relationship with your mom. When I lost a close friend of mine two years ago, I would go to this quiet place where we used to talk. Sometimes I'd sit there talking to her for hours. Reconnecting this way helped. It felt as if she was somehow still there. And she was, in my heart. Allowing myself to go through the pain made me see so clearly how much she contributed to my life.

"When your heart is broken it's difficult to find something to hold onto, something to be thankful for. The blessings of having a mom like yours seem empty when suddenly she's gone. Time has a way of making sense of what seems so senseless in the beginning, although it will take a while for the pain to subside before you can really smile about the good times you've had together and fully understand the invaluable lesson your mom left you. She showed you the importance of making a commitment to what matters in life, and to let nothing stand in the way of that.

"Once life gives you an ultimatum, it's a lot harder to put things in order. That's why it's the adults who are now making a clean sweep of their rooms, the neglected corners of their lives. The sting of those three little words, 'precious little time', has really hit home. There's no more putting off the decision of how we choose to live our lives. Holding onto shattered illusions of what we thought life should be only creates more pain.

"We're all learning to live with this lingering symptom called uncertainty. And you must feel so very uncertain right now without your mother here for support. But I know you will make it because when we're strong enough to share our pain, we heal. And when we learn to trust that all is well, that sets us free to enjoy life. The scars of living then become the marks of character, and character determines our destiny.

"You're already wise, Brent. Some day this pain will make you even wiser. We all go through pain to get there."

"But why do we have to suffer so much in the first place?" said Brent. "That's what I really want to know."

"There are some things in life that will always remain a paradox. And the pain of losing your mother deserves a greater explanation than I will ever be able to give. But maybe you can accept this. I learned that life isn't so much about fairness, as it is about meaning.

"When times seem the bleakest, that's when we see the greatness in people more clearly. We look at the ordinary with new eyes again, just like a child. Often the true heroes in life go unnoticed, until we're shown again how profoundly they affect our lives. It puts celebrity status into perspective when you see firemen and police officers running into burning buildings, risking their own lives to save others. Not a thought of race or religion stands in their way. Yet why should it take a catastrophe to see who the real heroes are, to shake us out of our complacency, and make us pay attention to the fact that we've gone off course?

"Maybe suffering is all part of a plan, a plan much larger than any of us can see. Maybe we go through pain to make it a greater journey home."

Brent raised his eyebrow with that look of teenage suspicion. "I don't think I quite get that 'journey home' bit."

I just smiled because neither did I for along time. "Sometimes when the answer goes over your head, you have to look above for it."

His eyes softened again.

"*I* think we suffer because that's how we finally come to be at home with ourselves. When we're truly who we're meant to be, there is no struggle. Just as a butterfly no longer struggles once it escapes the confines of its cocoon. It's the ultimate freedom for which we all long.

"The only question then becomes — are we willing to take the journey?"

*B*rent grew quiet. After a long pause he lifted his head, looked me straight in the eye and smiled back: "It's worth it... isn't it?"

"Yes," I said softly, with the pride I knew his mother would have felt. "It is."

Epilogue

We're all wounded in this life, each in different ways. It's part of the human condition. Sometimes, that pain and all it exposes become the source of our greatest strengths. And those strengths inevitably build a life of courage, wisdom and significance — a life that outlives us.

So I urge you to honor Brent's decision the next time you feel like giving up or say to yourself, "What's the use?" Know that in time, Brent, and others who will walk that same path, will make peace with the scars of life and turn them into the cornerstones of character.

May you take to heart what's true for you within this story and risk that journey. Make it worthwhile for yourself and the future adults of this world. Because if not you, who? There is no 'them'.

There is No THEM

How to Claim Yourself and Show Up in Your Life!

Learn how to apply the seven critical leadership, life management, and self-mastery principles with this dynamic, thought-provoking and transformative one-day program which includes:

• In-depth session on breaking through your invisible barriers to success to move you forward from where you are to where you want to be.

• Techniques for asking the right questions to rediscover yourself and build unshakeable self-assuredness to get what you want out of life.

• Powerful mind mastery techniques and rituals used by extraordinarily successful people to help you realize the results you deserve, financially and personally.

• How to tap into your greatest self-expression and combine success with significance.

• An advanced mind power technique to switch "on" your optimal power state at will.

Additional Bonus for you and your organization:
One half hour free coaching for each participant, or special group invitation to one of Dawn's seminars by teleconference.

Please Note: Limited dates available. Reserve well in advance to guarantee your space. An advanced two-day training is suggested after applying the principles for 90 days.

For details on this and other programs as well as customized conference and special event keynotes, please call toll free:
1 (866) 862-2438 or e-mail: dawn@dawnholman.com

ATTENTION:
Organizations, Schools and Corporate "Champions"
Book is available at substantial quantity discounts for community and educational fundraising, as well as for business cause marketing and promotional use. See contact information above for bulk orders.

About the Author and the Artist

An ever-evolving expert in the fields of leadership, life management, and self-mastery, Dawn is in constant demand by organizations seeking a content-rich yet masterful presenter. Whether serving as a keynote speaker, workshop leader or coach, her message transforms lives and restores commitment to "settle for more," regardless of life's uncertainties. She provides ready-to-implement strategies that propel people to greater levels of growth, success and personal fulfillment.

In creating her internationally acclaimed, award-winning series on cancer she had the privilege of interviewing extraordinary people around the world and became recognized as a popular media guest for her "collective" wisdom and poignant stories. Dawn knows, first-hand, the power of the unsinkable soul as well as the secrets of unleashing the internal power source to all life's riches. So whether you're stuck in a rut or raring to go, Dawn's profound and doable system to claim your best self will get you off the sidelines and into the game, big time.

Alexandra Morris first picked up a pencil at the age of three and has been drawing ever since. Amid the demands of Grade 12 studies, she took on the challenge of visually interpreting each page with uncanny insight for her 17 years of life experience, lending a purity and depth that could not otherwise have been achieved.

Dawn invites you, as a purchaser or corporate "champion" of There is No THEM , to visit www.dawnholman.com for your free Special Report (a $5.00 value). You may also wish to sign up for her regular monthly articles as a way to continue cementing the concepts and practices from her workshops, or as an introduction to the path of lifework and personal mastery. Either way, you will have access to leading edge concepts and practical wisdom in the vast arena of human potential, growth and evolution — content you can apply immediately to improve the quality of your life!

We Have a Request

Dawn would love to hear how this book has affected your life and those around you. We encourage you to share your stories and insights. Or maybe you have a tip or quote you'd like to pass along to other readers through her articles and Special Reports? Dawn guarantees to respond with a personal note. We're listening!

You can contact Dawn at: 1 (866) 862-2438
or e-mail: dawn@dawnholman.com